Twenty Something

Written by: Amber J. Graham

© 2016 US Copyright Office. All rights reserved.

Table of Contents

Twenty Something 1

From the Author 7

Build It 13

Self-Reflection… 18

Love To Love 21

Love Check… 25

Yours…Mine…Ours 27

Just Write! 31

Change 36

Self-Check… 40

Let Go 43

Are You Free? 47

Forgiveness 50

Write About It! 54

Life Goes On 56

Just Write! 60

Be Yourself 62

Question Time… 66

Laugh More 69

Remember the Time? 72

Fess Up 76

Moment of Truth... 78

Walk Before You Run 80

Building Blocks... 83

Time 86

Freeze 88

Alone Time 90

Turn It Off 92

Prayers Up 94

Prayers 97

Acquire Knowledge 99

Self-Check... 103

Money Train 106

Add It Up... 109

Something New 112

Try it... 114

Carry On 118

Notes 121

Chapters 153

From the Author

I recently turned twenty-five and I'm most certainly not where my eighteen year old self thought I would be. My eighteen year old self just knew that by now I would be married, well into my career and putting together my first movie script. Well, at-least something along those lines. Instead, I'm single, without children, doing the furthest thing from my dream career. I realize that when you're eighteen life seems simple, you think you have it all figured out, you think you're grown. At eighteen you're ready to conquer the world and you feel invincible. I realize now, that at eighteen I was very naïve. It is almost as if you live in this fairy tale bubble. As you get older, that spark slowly seems to disappear. You move further away from your dreams because adulthood tends to override what you truly desire, you get confused. You feel bombarded with responsibilities and important life-changing decisions. Often times, people try to push their reality off on you, pushing you to believe that your aspirations are unrealistic and mediocre. Nonetheless, you have to fight. Fight for your dreams and for the life that you want. Fight for your happiness and joy. Fight for your goals, fight for love, and fight for your beliefs. Stand tall for the things that you believe in, but don't be afraid to look beyond your own perspective.

For years I beat myself up over not being where I should be, but I realize now that I'm exactly where I'm supposed to be. We can't rush God's timing and what is meant for us will always be for us, no person or thing on this earth can take that away. I had to stop trying to force myself to achieve what others had done. I had to stop comparing myself to other people and I had to learn to stop trying to do things without God.

I wanted to write this book to give people something to relate to, especially people struggling to find their way. I wanted to step away from fictional writing and write something from the heart, something personal.

Build It

I've worked several jobs over the past four or five years, none of those jobs dealt directly with what I actually want to do in life. I'm not even sure what my ultimate career goal is. Once upon a time I wanted to be a Juvenile Defense Attorney. I also thought that I wanted to be a teacher. I know that writing is my passion and it is the only thing that I can see myself doing and being happy doing, even if the pay wasn't great.

Over the course of my adult years I have merely worked to make a living. I liked some positions, some better than others, but at the end of the day, I was only working to make money. None of the jobs made me happy and they weren't professions that I could see myself retiring from. It wasn't until I got more in tune with the Word of God that I realized my jobs were not my mission.

For so long I let every job that I held take away from my passion of writing and my overall happiness. I understand that we sometimes have to hold down certain titles and man odd end positions to survive, but at what cost are we surviving? We dedicate so much of our time to making money and helping companies become more successful, but we don't dedicate nearly as much time to building our own brands, dreams and futures.

A lot of people share the same desire to be wealthy and there's nothing wrong with being wealthy. However, is wealth ultimately going to keep you mentally and spiritually fed? Is money going to keep you happy even though you hate what you are doing? If so, more power to you. But, for most of us, the answer to those two questions is no.

Personally, I would rather do what I love and make less money, opposed to doing something that I hate because it pays well and it is satisfying my financial greed. Maybe what I love doing won't make me as wealthy as other career ventures, but that is a chance that I'm willing to take. I've spent the last few years of my life feeding monetary desires all while starving my dreams, that route hasn't gotten me very far and it certainly hasn't kept me happy and I'm currently far from satisfied.

Every time I walk by a book store I wish my book was on one of the shelves. Every time I watch a movie, I wish my name was in the credits. I've prayed to be a successful writer. I've prayed to have my book become a New York Times

Bestseller. It wasn't until recently that I came to the understanding that God would allow my vision and prayers to come to pass, but I have to do my part. I have to stay focused and maintain a strong level of faith. Just as I work to earn my pay check every two weeks, I have to work to earn my vision. The ball has always been in my court, I've just been afraid to take my shot. I've sacrificed sleep, holidays and so much more for corporations, but not for the things that I have a deeply embedded desire to accomplish. At twenty-five that had to stop.

Do your job and do it to the best of your abilities, but stop dedicating so much of yourself to your job that you neglect your purpose. While you are at work, work hard but work even harder for God and for yourself. If you want to be the CEO of your own company pray for it, work for it, study what it takes to be a CEO and dedicate yourself to doing what it takes to see your goals come to pass. Listen to God, trust in His plan and rely on His understanding; trust in His timing, not your own. Do not sell yourself short, finish what you start and remain humble through success and failure.

    You can spend your life working for someone else, perhaps that will make you rich and perhaps that will keep you satisfied. For the rest us, we have to cast down our doubts, believe in what we're working towards and we cannot become discouraged by what tries to weigh us down. Do not settle for anything less than what has been promised to you. Always keep in mind that you either walk in faith or you walk in fear; you can't walk in both. Life itself is a virtue and always remember that this is your marathon, no one elses.

Self-Reflection...

Answer the questions below.

Be open and honest with yourself.

What is your ideal career?

_____

_____

_____

_____

Will the career you listed above make you happy? Why or why not?

_____

_____

_____

_____

_____

What would you want to do for the rest of your life if money wasn't a factor?

_____

_____

_____

_____

_____

What do you think your gifts are?

_____

_____

_____

_____

Does your gift connect with your ideal career? Why or why not?

_____

_____

_____

_____

Love To Love

I've had my share of heart breaks. I've mistaken lust for love. I've loved the wrong people for the wrong reasons. I've been used and betrayed by people who have claimed to love me. I've even loved when I wasn't loved in return. Through all of that, I've learned how powerful love can be. I've seen how love can change people and how it forces people to grow and to mature. I've also witnessed how strong love actually is. Love can break down barriers and heal wounds. Love is more than a theory; love is unwavering. Love doesn't keep a score book of rights and wrongs. Love is seen in our actions and in how we treat one another. Love is more than just a word, love is demonstrated in our behavior. Love isn't easily provoked, nor is it easily broken.

If you don't do anything else while you roam this earth…love. First of all, love God and love yourself. Understand how much God loves you and take heed to what being embraced by His love means. Grow an understanding of how powerful His love for you is. Once you embrace the love of God, master self-love and learn to love people. Learn to love the unlovable; usually they are the people who need love the most. Embrace love from other people and don't deny others the opportunity to love you.

It was a close friend of mine that taught me how to love, and how to be patient and kind when loving. He and I met when I was sixteen, he was nineteen. I was very rough around the edges and spoiled. I was dismissive towards the idea of loving someone and I avoided expressing my emotions. At the time, I had never loved by anyone other than relatives and a few close friends. But, even by loving them, my love had not been stretched. It was him who taught me what it meant to truly love someone.

He taught me what it meant to love someone selflessly, even when it is difficult. I learned to let go of expectations, true love doesn't have expectations. He was far from someone that I thought I would fall in love with, but I did. Love doesn't recognize fleshly attractions. He taught me to love him as he was and to stop trying to fix him. Love is acceptance, flaws and all. He taught me to love fearlessly; to not be in fear of being hurt. Love shouldn't be a fear based emotion. Although we are no longer together we are still close friends and his love will always be deeply embedded in my heart. He taught me that love is not only an emotion, it's an action. Above all, he taught me that I could love him or anyone else for that matter without continuing a relationship because love is and always will be, unconditional. Love has no room for jealously or envy. Love is patient and kind. Love is a feeling of protection. Love is blind and doesn't care whether you are poor or wealthy, beautiful or hideous. Love is sometimes ugly, yet always beautiful.

Love will not always be easy, but love is one of the most beautiful things we can extend to ourselves and to each other. We must learn to stop hiding behind fear and to step out on a limb and love; love freely, and openly.

Love Check...

What does love mean to you?

_____

_____

_____

_____

_____

What do you love about yourself?

_____

_____

_____

_____

_____

Do you fear anything about loving other people?

_____

_____

_____

_____

_____

Yours...Mine...Ours

Every relationship, romantic or otherwise must be built on a strong foundation. I've always believed that relationships need some of the same components, trust, communication, and honesty in order to flourish.

Trust: Understand that people are just that, people. They're bound to make mistakes and it is inevitable that they will do idiotic things. Even though we as people make mistakes we should never intentionally cause harm to others whether emotional, mental or physical, but especially to the people that trust us. I've always believed that you shouldn't ask from people what you can't give, therefore trust is not one sided. Do not expect a person to trust you when its apparent that you do not trust them. Above all, never put more trust in a person than you put into God, that will always lead to disappointment.

Communication: So many things go wrong in relationships because people fail to communicate. If you don't like when someone does something, tell them. If someone made you mad, tell them. People walk around irate at their friends, spouses or whomever, without ever actually telling them. Learn to communicate, in the long run it will clarify misunderstandings and strengthen the relationship. Also, we live in an era of technology and with that social media networks are not an appropriate method of expressing yourself to a person. If you have a disagreement with someone, talk it out, don't text, tweet or Facebook it…you don't need an audience to speak your truth.

Honesty: I will keep it simple. Be honest with people. Be honest about how you feel and tell the truth. Sometimes the truth is a hard pill to swallow but it is a necessary remedy.

Do not remain in relationships and/or friendships where you are constantly giving and aren't getting anything in return. Relationships are 100/100, give a little, and take a little. Giving can be lending support and an array of other things, it doesn't always have to be something tangible. Appreciate one another and continue to work hard to keep the relationship strong, just as you did to establish it.

I recently lost a close friend because we failed to communicate. We engaged in a social media dispute, opposed to speaking face to face. Text messages were miscommunicated and we put our pride above our friendship. At some point we stopped being truthful with one another and we lost the trust that we once established. While she and I will probably never rekindle our friendship, she taught me a lot about bonds. She taught me how easily it is to grow apart from people and how easily it is to become detached from people because of miscommunications. As you get older and throughout stages of personal growth you will outgrow people simply because everyone can't go where you are going. Nonetheless, do not give up on people so easily. Pick your battles wisely and always fight for those who are worth fighting for.

Just Write!

Change

Change is growth. In life we're all after something different. We have diverse goals and ambitions. Often times we must embrace change in order to reach new heights. Most people fear change because of the uncertainty and discomfort that it brings. Sometimes change is scary and uncertainty is even scarier. But, not knowing what is yet to come, taking chances and trying things outside of our comfort zones is how we grow and how we evolve. We must learn to enjoy and appreciate the process of change. Appreciate the sense of adventure that it brings. Roll with the punches and concentrate on all of the amazing outcomes that change can bring. If we do not change, how can we expect to experience new and better things? Honestly, we can't.

I moved from Detroit, Michigan to North Olmsted, Ohio. For the first time in my life I lived more than thirty minutes away from my friends and my family, all of the people that I have known my entire life. I was going on twenty-four at the time and I was very timid towards change. I moved to a new city with a small amount of money, no furniture and a lot of doubt in my decisions. For a long period of time I didn't want to embrace anything, not Ohio, not the people and most certainly not the new journey that I was beginning. I was at a standstill. I was scared to embrace anything. I wanted to click my heels and be back in Detroit with the things and people that I was familiar with. Almost against my will I had to push myself to break free of the life that I had in Detroit. I learned to accept that I had to take ownership of my new life and my new surroundings and eventually I did. By doing this, I let go of so many bad habits and so much emotional weight. I gained a new perspective of myself and my goals. I grew closer to God and strengthened my faith. I met amazing people and pushed myself to step outside of my comfort zone. I outgrew a lot of people and situations. By embracing change and such a transition, I found pieces of myself that were buried. I found pieces of myself that I never knew existed.

Imagine if you never changed after high school. Imagine surrounding yourself with the same people, committing to the same habits and same routines. Imagine if you dressed the same, spoke the same and thought the same as you did when you were sixteen. You would be stuck in a past time, while the people and things around you were evolving and moving forward. The world is constantly changing and sometimes we must change with it. We must experience new things and sometimes rid ourselves of old things. Do not fear the unknown and do not be afraid to embrace it. There is so much goodness hidden in change, don't wrap yourself in fears arms clinching to past times.

Self-Check...

Who were you five years ago?

_____

_____

_____

_____

_____

Who are you today?

_____

_____

_____

_____

_____

How have you changed?

_____
_____
_____
_____
_____

Who have you grown apart from?

_____
_____
_____
_____
_____

What habits have you grown out of?

_____

_____

_____

_____

What habits have your grown into?

_____

_____

_____

_____

Let Go

We can't undo our actions and even though we can recant statements, words can't be unheard. Our lives are not Facebook statues, we can't edit mistakes and remove errors. The past is the past. You can't change what happened yesterday or an hour ago, don't spend your time focusing on it. We're human, we make mistakes, and we sometimes speak before we think. We're bound to both do and say hurtful and sometimes thoughtless things.

There have been times when I beat myself up over things that I've done or things that I wished I hadn't done, but over time I learned that my past and my mistakes don't determine my tomorrows. If you are too busy looking back, you'll miss all of the goodness in front of you.

It took me a very long time and I meant a very long time to comprehend what letting go meant and the freedom that came with it. I sent my first book to a publisher, and never heard anything back. I was this bright eyed, bushy tailed author until what I thought at the time was Dooms Day occurred. I don't know if someone read the book, or if it was just discarded. For a great deal of time I held onto that disappointment. I was crushed. I became doubtful of myself and of my writing. For a while I even stopped writing, I no longer saw a point in the stories and messages I was trying to convey. Thankfully, I came to my senses. It literally took me years, but I overcame what I thought was the end to my writing career. I watched a video of Tyler Perry and it reminded me of something. You'll experience disappointment, rejection, pain and an array of other things. But, you have to let go and you have to move forward. It took time for me to take heed to his message, but eventually it hit me like a slap in the face. I realized that the best was yet to come. Maybe the publisher didn't like my book, but I couldn't allow one door closing to prevent me from standing in the threshold of other doors. I made the decision to keep writing and to keep putting my thoughts into the atmosphere. I had to knock down the barriers that I had allowed myself to build.

If you are angry about something today, don't give it power to ruin your tomorrows. More importantly, if you've let something go, do not allow other people to keep trying to beat you over the head with it. Who you were a month ago doesn't have to be who you are today. You can determine to wake up regretting the things that you did yesterday, or you can wake up with a positive attitude and aim to be and to do better. Master letting the past go, make peace with it and move on. Your future is bright, do not let the past dim your light. You'll continue to make mistakes. Somedays you'll get discouraged. When you fall, get back up. When you do something wrong, figure out where you went wrong and learn from it. Stop confining yourself to humanly mistakes, stop allowing other people to define you by your mistakes. Keep moving forward, it is your marathon, stop trying to run it backwards, stop trying to pace yourself with another person's speed. Lastly, stay in constant practice of letting go, letting go of the things that are binding you to a past time, mistake or bad situation.

Are You Free?

Use this space to write about what you need to let go of to be free.

_____

_____

_____

_____

_____

_____

_____

_____

_____

_____

_____

How do you intend to free yourself?

Why is it important to free yourself?

Forgiveness

Forgiveness is one of the hardest things in life to master, not only forgiving others but forgiving ourselves. It wasn't until recently that I began to understand why it is important to forgive both other people and ourselves. There were times when individuals did something to me that I didn't appreciate and I held onto the frustration and anger. I became very passive aggressive. Meanwhile, they were living their life not putting any thought into why my face was twisted up. I would literally be mad for days at people that had no clue why I was angry. There were even times when I was upset with myself. I couldn't sleep, I had headaches and I kept over-thinking of ways to resolve the wrongs I had created.

I had to learn how to forgive people and let situations rest for the sake of my own happiness and health. I also had to learn how to forgive myself and stop beating myself up over things I had done in error. Forgiveness is for your own peace. Being completely honest, God will take care of our troubles. We don't have to walk around mad at folks ready to fight every opportunity that we get. God will settle the matter once we do our part. As His children, when we forgive people He will put it on their hearts to apologize. Amazing, right?

A few years ago my boyfriend and I broke up. He felt that I didn't have enough time for him because I was working two jobs and going to school. According to him, he felt neglected, therefor he cheated. Having both of our best interests in mind, we decided not to get back together. A part of me hated him for a very long time. I hated him for breaking my trust and for destroying whatever future we may have had. But mostly, I hated him for tainting my trust and my perspective towards love and relationships. Over the years we spoke from time to time and would spend time together, but I never forgave him. I never forgave myself for allowing his actions to affect my future relationships with people and other men. I had trust issues and any time I attempted to be in a relationship with another person I assumed they were cheating or weren't being honest. I was bitter. Deep down I was looking for an apology that I never was going to receive. I was tired of fighting an emotional battle, meanwhile he had moved on with someone else. I began to ask God to help me find forgiveness. I asked God to help me forgive myself. It took some time but I found peace and forgave both him and myself.

Don't be stubborn towards forgiveness. Find it in your heart to forgive those who have wronged you. Forgiveness means you no longer desire revenge and you no longer have a chip on your shoulder about the person's actions. When you forgive people, you don't have to force yourself to maintain communication and/or relationships with them, but at-least free yourself from spirits of resentment and anger. Do not spend your life holding onto a burden that isn't yours to bear.

Write About It!

Who do you need to forgive?

_____

_____

_____

_____

_____

Why is forgiving the above person and/or people difficult for you?

_____

_____

_____

_____

_____

How will you work on forgiving people?

_____

_____

_____

_____

_____

Life Goes On

Growing up and leading into my adult years, I didn't handle rejection well. I didn't and couldn't handle things not going my way. I could have the upmost confidence until a person told me no, then I was ready to shut down and run home to my parents. I hated being turned down or not being able to get things that I felt I deserved. One day I was humbled and I realized that life goes on and sometimes what we think we deserve isn't what we've actually earned. We can also think we deserve something when in actuality we deserve something even better.

When I was eighteen or nineteen years old I worked for Home Depot and one day out of the clear blue sky I was fired for stealing. I knew I hadn't stolen anything and I was wrongfully terminated from my position. I had never stolen anything in life, other than snacks from Latchkey, I apologize Ms. T!

I was out of a job and my pride was hurt for being accused of something that I knew I hadn't done. I cried. I was livid. I was hurt and insulted. I wanted to set the store on fire. I wanted to fight the people who had accused me. Several scenarios went through my head. My mother was the only person who assured me that something better was going to come along. She reminded of how hard I worked and how intelligent I was. She reminded me that I had my whole life ahead of me and that Home Depot was just another pit stop. Low and behold, a few weeks later a company that I had previously worked for called me with a job offer. I not only would be making more money than I was at Home Depot, but I was going to be exposed to greater opportunities. Yes, I had been knocked down but it wasn't long before I was picked back up. The situation became one of those "ah,ha" moments.

Life isn't fair and you won't always get your way. Sometimes you'll be over looked for that raise or promotion that you've worked your butt off for. Sometimes people will reject you before they even get the chance to know you. And, sometimes the most unfair things will happen to you without reason. Nonetheless, I promise you, life goes on. Sometimes things don't go our way because something or someone even better is going to come along. We occasionally lose things to gain something even greater. You have to learn to take things in stride. To carry on and stop questioning why certain things happen to you and not other people. You can't shut down and give up when things don't go your way. Remain humble and be patient, everything that is meant for you will come in due time. I'll say it again, nobody and nothing on this planet can rob you of what God has already said is for you.

    Remember two things:

Success is perspectival and everything happens for a reason.

Just Write!

Be Yourself

You are going to meet a lot of people throughout your life. You will have your fair share of friendships and relationships. You'll be forced to impress people and play nice for employers, sometimes you may even have to play hardball with your co-workers. While meeting and getting to know people you will realize that some individuals will like you and others won't. Some people won't have valid reasons as to why they don't like you, they just won't like you.

I've never been one who tries to impress people by being someone that I'm not. I grew up with the understanding that I wasn't for everyone. My mother frequently reminds me that what others think of me is none of my business. I've always been the weird one, the outspoken one and the one who doesn't care much about what others have to say about me. Meanwhile, people give me the ugly stare because they don't agree with or understand who I am and that is perfectly fine.

I'm six feet tall, even if I could change my height, I wouldn't. I'd be telling a lie if I said I've always been comfortable with my height because I haven't. Over the years I had to grow to accept and love the fact that I'm tall. I wasn't always comfortable with my gap either. I once thought that it was ugly and that it made me ugly. Even at twenty-five people still try to taunt me about it. I've learned to love it. I don't see it as a flaw. I view my gap as something that makes me unique. After all, how many people can shoot water through their teeth? I've worked hard to love myself and I will not let anyone or anything make me feel like I am not good enough or as if I need to change myself to be liked.

My point is, despite who does or doesn't like you, be yourself and you will attract the right people. Don't try to put on facades to appease others. Allow people the chance to get to know and love you for who you are and if they don't, so be it. I've seen people try to become the complete opposite of who they are to get someone's attention. I've also seen people change themselves so much to please other people that they no longer recognize themselves. You will meet people who have suggestions about things you should do to yourself to become a better person. There will probably even be times that you have to compromise certain things about yourself perhaps for work or for your relationship and that's okay. But, at the end of the day, do not let other people try to modify who you are, only to make you the person that they want you to be. There is always room for self-improvement, nonetheless stand strong and take pride in yourself.

Question Time...

What do you like about yourself?

_____
_____
_____
_____
_____

What do you dislike about yourself?

_____
_____
_____
_____
_____

Who you are?

_____

_____

_____

_____

Are you confident in who you are?

_____

_____

_____

_____

Are there any areas of your life that need improvement?

_____

_____

_____

_____

What is your plan of action to improve?

_____

_____

_____

_____

_____

Laugh More

With so much going on around us, it is rather easy to become discouraged. Sometimes you just need a hearty chuckle. Life is too precious and far too short not to enjoy it. We must laugh and laugh often, laughter is one of the best remedies to adversity.

There have been times when I've wanted to cry but instead I chose to laugh. There have also been times when I've wanted to get angry but instead I chose to laugh. Sometimes I'm even forced to laugh at myself. On several occasions I've laughed so hard that other people have laughed without even knowing what I was laughing at, that's how contagious laughter is.

There was a time in my life where everything was going wrong. My job gave me two weeks' notice that they were closing. Someone very close to me had been sentenced to five years in prison. I was having financial issues and had no choice but to move back in with my parents. They were in the mist of looking for a home therefore I felt stuck. I found out that my aunt had brain cancer. On top of all of that, my dad was about to have open heart surgery. It was a difficult time for both me and my family. It was laughter that kept us sane. It was laughter that temporarily made us forget about the mayhem going on around us. Looking back, I can laugh at how frantic I was because God made a way. My dad is alive and well, my finances are much better, my friend will be getting released from prison this year and although my aunt passed away, she is no longer in pain.

Laughing decreases blood pressure, decreases stress and increases blood flow. Sometimes a good giggle is all we need. Don't take everything so seriously and stop taking everything personally.

Remember the Time?

Think about a time you got really angry or sad. Was it that serious? Is the situation funny now?

_____

_____

_____

_____

_____

_____

_____

_____

_____

_____

Fess Up

I know, I know, this will be a tough one but you can do it! Admit when you're wrong. Admit when you need help. Admit when you miss people. It is okay to be honest with yourself and with others.

In the past, I never wanted to admit when people were right, when I was wrong or when I needed help. When I had my first apartment I would go days without eating because I was too prideful to admit that I needed assistance. I kept myself suffering because I didn't want to confess to anyone, not even to God that I was struggling. I finally admitted to my bestfriend at the time that I was struggling and although she didn't have much herself, she gave me food. She went with me to look for jobs and she did what she could to help me maintain. Looking back, that was pretty stupid of me to do. Back then I didn't comprehend that even though it would be difficult to admit that I needed help, it was even more of a challenge to struggle when there was help for me to receive.

I know asking for help can be difficult and I know admitting when you are wrong can be even more difficult, but it isn't impossible. As people, we have to learn to put our pride aside and admit to our errors and prideful ways. Sometimes we have to lose in order to win.

Moment of Truth...

Is there anything that you need to own up to?

Be candid!

_____

_____

_____

_____

_____

_____

_____

_____

_____

_____

_____

_____

Walk Before You Run

I have to remind myself of this, take life one day at a time. We can be so hard on ourselves because we aren't living the life we expected to be living by the time that we expected to be living it. Maybe you aren't where you want to be today, but one day you will be. Maybe you don't have as much money saved as you would like, but one day you will. Rome wasn't built in a day and you won't get everything you want and be exactly where you want to be in one day either.

I have spent most of my twenties trying to get somewhere when I didn't even know where I was trying to go. I have always set my sight on the destination and not the journey. I have tried so hard to accomplish all of my dreams at once that I've barely accomplished any of them. I had to learn to plant one seed at a time and allow it to flourish before trying to plant another. I also had to learn to deal with disappointment and the reality that my plans are going to change. The road ahead is not always straight, sometimes we will encounter multiple hurdles before we even come close to where we're trying to go.

Sometimes we get so caught up in making the right decisions that we end up making the wrong ones. One bad decision could ruin your life but it doesn't have to. You're exactly where you need to be and you'll get exactly where you are supposed to be, just give it time.

One day at a time, you'll figure it out! Please stop using drugs, shopping, money, sex and/or whatever else to cope with life when things get difficult. The best way to overcome moments of doubt, struggle and disappointment is to just face

them head on.

Building Blocks...

At this very moment, how did you expect your life to be?

_____
_____
_____
_____
_____

What is the reality of your life?

_____
_____
_____
_____
_____

What is your plan to get where you want be?

_____

_____

_____

_____

Do you have a five year plan?

_____

_____

_____

_____

Do you often reevaluate your five year plan?

_____

_____

_____

_____

How do you deal with disappointment?

_____

_____

_____

_____

Time

Sadly, I learned to appreciate time with the passing of my grandmother. I was always going to visit her tomorrow. I was always going to call her tomorrow. One day, tomorrow never came for her. One day tomorrow never came for us. I was too consumed with trivial things that I neglected to make time for her. I neglected to appreciate the time that I did have with her. I've learned to value the time that I spend with my loved ones and I try to make every moment count.

Time is one of the most valuable, yet priceless things that we have. We don't know how much time we have on this earth, only God knows that. Spend your time wisely. Invest your time in experiences and in people, not things. Go with the flow, don't let trivial issues distract you from what matters most. Take a few moments every day to reflect and to be thankful. Live each day in the moment and live each day to the fullest. Spend time doing what you love, spend time with the people who are most important to you and never take the time that you are given for granted. Be cautious about who you give your time to and what you put your time into. For a lack of better words, everything isn't deserving of your time. Be gracious about time that you are given, it's one of the most precious gifts that we will ever receive.

Freeze

How do you spend most of your time?

_____

_____

_____

_____

_____

Who do you need to spend more time with?

_____

_____

_____

_____

_____

What do you need to spend more of your time doing?

_____

_____

_____

_____

_____

_____

_____

Alone Time

I spend a lot of time on social media websites and it seems like everybody spends the majority of their time talking about how alone they are. Sometimes I get a little lonely too, but when that happens I find something to occupy my time or my mind. Whether it's going to the movies, to the park or out to a new restaurant. I do something. I believe that it's important to experience and venture out on your own. At first you may resent doing things solo, but once you actually go to the movies for the first time alone or to the park, you'll feel liberated. You don't always need to be around other people to boost your happiness. Take some time to yourself and discover your hobbies, your likes and your interests then maybe you can share those things with someone else.

Don't underestimate the power of your own company and don't rely so heavily on others that you can't appreciate being in the company of yourself.

Turn It Off

What do you like to do alone?

_____
_____
_____
_____

When is the last time you spent time alone doing something you enjoy?

_____
_____
_____
_____

When and what was the last time you did something for the first time?

Prayers Up

I'm not ashamed to admit that I didn't discover the power of prayer until my twenties, more so until I was twenty-four. Growing up my mother would always make us pray before she would pull out of the drive-way, I didn't understand why, and I found it rather annoying. As I got older I began to understand why we prayed, but I still hadn't grasped the power of prayer. I understand now that she made us pray to keep us protected, to keep us covered in the blood of Jesus. She made us pray to assure that we made it to our destinations safely and unharmed. I don't think I've ever told her this, but I'm thankful. I'm thankful for those prayers. I'm thankful that she trained us to put our faith in God and not into ourselves or others despite our decision making abilities.

Over the past few years I've felt like I was under attack and I started to pray. I started reading my Bible more often and I noticed things began to change. I discerned a change in myself, more so now than ever. I came to understand that God wasn't only listening to my prayers, He was answering them.

I'm still learning, but prayer has taught me to be patient, to put my trust in His promises. It is important to pray for yourself and for others. Always be mindful of your prayers and open to receiving what you've prayed for. Get in the habit of praying when you are happy, when you are sad, when you are strong, when you are weak. Give thanks to God and don't only seek Him when you are in need of something, seek Him just to give thanks, just to touch basis. God is the best person to call on when we need someone to talk to, when we feel down and out and when we feel like we are on top of the world. Be patient when you pray, and have faith in God and in the power of your words.

Prayers

What or who do you pray for the most?

_____

_____

_____

_____

_____

Do you have faith in your prayers?

_____

_____

_____

_____

_____

How do you think praying has helped you?

Acquire Knowledge

Quite honestly, after high school I didn't want to go to college. I wanted to jump right into the work force and figure out what it was that I wanted out of life. I felt pressured to go to school, so I did. I attended Wayne State University and wasted almost two years doing absolutely nothing. I took two classes a semester before I decided to call it quits. After that I attended the University of Phoenix and obtained my Associate's Degree in Liberal Arts. If you remember, I mentioned that at one point I wanted to be a Juvenile Defense Attorney but I knew me and Law School wouldn't get along. After I obtained my Associate's I entered my Bachelor's program. I was unenthusiastic and became very lazy in my studies. I decided to take another break from school. I eventually changed jobs and ended up getting one of the biggest slaps in the face of my life. I couldn't apply for the position that I wanted because I didn't have a Bachelor's Degree. I was offended and I was angry, my job history proved that I could do the job, nonetheless my educational background or lack thereof proved otherwise. That was all the motivation that I needed. I immediately re-enrolled in school to peruse my Bachelor's Degree at Cleveland State University. It is a bitter reality when you can't do something that you know you are qualified to do because you don't have the degree backing your experience.

I'm not sure why I despise college so much because I enjoy learning, perhaps I appreciate self-educating more than I do traditional education. I guess college was just never something I thought I needed in my deck of cards. I realize that in this day and age, without a college education you won't excel in certain fields, regardless of how qualified you are for the position.

I can't preach going to college, after all it took me from the age of eighteen to twenty-four to finally dedicate myself. Nonetheless, I will speak from experience. Don't rush into a major but start college if it is truly what you desire. Get your prerequisites out of the way and then decide a major. The longer you prolong going to college the more resistant you will become. Also don't allow others to bully you into a decision, make the decision about college or whatever it is that you want to do with your life for yourself.

I've also realized that certain fields will always be prominent and others will not, but don't let that stop you from studying your desired field.

Above all, feed your brain. Your brain is one of your greatest weapons. Don't only obtain information, gain an understanding for what you are learning. We often times confuse education with knowledge and knowledge with wisdom. Don't believe everything that you see and read, do your own research, seek your own truths. You've heard it time and time again, knowledge is power!

Don't ever stop learning. Continue to fuel your brain with knowledge, learn from other people and from everything around you.

Self-Check...

What was the last book you read?

_____
_____
_____
_____
_____

How do you learn on an ordinary basis?

_____
_____
_____
_____
_____

What do you want to learn more about?

_____

_____

_____

_____

What are you most knowledgeable about?

_____

_____

_____

_____

_____

_____

What are you ignorant to?

_____
_____
_____
_____

How often do you use your acquired knowledge?

_____
_____
_____
_____
_____

Money Train

I've went through several financial phases in my life. At one point I was a penny pincher and at another I blew money like there was no tomorrow. I got into a financial rut, I had credit card bills that I couldn't pay and all of my bills began to pile up. Sadly, I was using one credit card to pay for another. On pay day I paid bills then spent the rest of my earnings with friends, going out to eat or buying liquor. One day I got tired. I was tired of debt collectors calling me. I was tired of receiving threatening letters in the mail. At twenty-four I wised up and paid all of my credit cards off and canceled them with the exception of one. I learned to go out less and save more, I had to, I was drowning. I'm proud to say that I am debt free, other than student loans and I've learned to save money and stay far away from credit card offers.

Money seems to have the greatest material presence in our lives, at-least for me it has. With that being said, learn how to budget. Instead of eating out all of the time, cook. Budget your spending. If you know you have bills to pay or other important financial business that requires your attention, don't spend aimlessly and unnecessarily. Open a savings account and put money in it every time you get paid. Learn to save money! You don't have to spend every dollar you earn. I promise it won't burn a hole through your pocket.

If you find yourself getting offer after offer from credit card companies, it's okay to turn them down. If you do decide to take credit card agreements remember that you are responsible for paying back what you spend, it may seem like free money but it's not. Debt is not something to look forward to. You want to build your credit, not destroy it. Don't take on more financial responsibilities than you can afford, stay in your financial lane. When I say stay in your financial lane, I mean don't try to keep up with the Jones's, don't spend money you really don't have, don't spend your last trying to impress or appease people. I've had times where I just blew money just because I had it, but in the end I was left looking and feeling foolish because I didn't save anything. It is okay to spend money and buy nice things…after all you worked for it, but always keep in mind that you need to spend wisely.

Add It Up...

What do you spend the majority of your money on?

_____

_____

_____

_____

How much money do you spend on average?

_____

_____

_____

_____

What do you waste a lot of money on?

_____

_____

_____

_____

How often do you go out?

(Movies, Dinner, Etc.)

_____

_____

_____

_____

How much money would you like to save per month?

_____
_____
_____
_____

What habits do you need to break in order to meet your monthly savings goal?

_____
_____
_____
_____

Something New

I've stuck to my comfort zone for most of my life. If it was something new, I automaticity would say that I didn't like it. It wasn't until one of my friends gave me a reality check. She asked me," Amber, how can you say you don't like something if you've never tried it?" I didn't respond. I honestly didn't have an answer or at-least a legitimate one. The ironic thing was, that wasn't the first time I had been asked the question, but it was the first time I actually thought about the question.

I started to try new things, new foods and new activities. I gradually started to break free from my comfort zone. At the age of twenty-five I realized how much I wasn't experiencing because I wasn't indulging in anything new. I discovered a love for so many things that I had turned my back on in the past. I know certain foods sound disgusting or you think certain activities sound uninteresting, but try them before you make up your mind. Explore unfamiliar places, try food from other cultures, and listen to music outside of your customary genres. You might surprise yourself at some of the things that you like.

Try it...

Try something new and write about.

What did you try? How did it make you feel? Will you do it again? What do you want to try next?

_____
_____
_____
_____
_____
_____
_____
_____
_____
_____

Carry On

As I continue to navigate my way through life, I realize that I still have so much more to learn and so much more to see. I have my entire life ahead of me. I've learned to be independent, moving to Ohio taught me that. I've learned that life doesn't always go as planned, everyday situations have taught me that. I had to learn to adjust to situations. Sometimes you just have to go with the flow and always trust that God is going to catch you when you fall. Oddly enough, I learned how to cry and how to say goodbye. I learned that with every ending is a new beginning. I learned to say no without feeling the need to explain myself. I found myself and I'm still finding pieces of myself. My twenties have taught me how to love myself, how to take advantage of opportunities when they come and how to free myself of the burdens and baggage I've been carrying for so many years. My twenties have taught me to stop walking in fear, to stop doubting myself and to most importantly trust God.

People will probably tell you that your twenties are a time to make mistakes, a time to grow and learn. That may be true, but you have the choice to make these years whatever you wish them to be. You'll probably hear that these are the best years of your life and they should be, but shouldn't ever year be? You'll make a lot of mistakes and you'll learn a lot of lessons. Some days you'll feel like you are stuck and some days you'll feel like you're on top of the world. You might find love, you might not. You might lose your way a few times, but you'll eventually find it. People will continue to test your life decisions, they'll tease you about your age and you'll constantly hear," ah, it's okay, you're still young." You'll be judged, you'll lose friends and you'll make friends. You'll want to give up. You'll probably even regret a few things. You'll be scared sometimes and others you'll have the heart of a lion. You'll work weird jobs and probably dislike most of your employers. Some days you might break down and ask yourself the what's the point of it all, but through everything just breathe. You've got this!

Notes

Chapters

As you grow throughout your twenties and throughout the rest of your life, appreciate both old and new chapters. Appreciate the experiences that you've had and the people that you've met. Take negatives situations in stride and rejoice in your victories. Live your life; do not be afraid to start over nor to rebuild. Sometimes it is in your weakest moments that you will find your greatest strength. If you fall down 101 times get back up 102. Every day is a new page to a chapter in your book, keep writing your chapters, keep growing and keep persevering.

Love and peace,

Amber J

www.ingramcontent.com/pod-product-compliance
Lightning Source LLC
Chambersburg PA
CBHW020905090426
42736CB00008B/502